Joseph Ato Forson

The Distributional Effect of Social Welfare Spending in an Economy: Evidence from Thailand

Document Nr. V210953

Joseph Ato Forson

The Distributional Effect of Social Welfare Spending in an Economy: Evidence from Thailand

GRIN Verlag

Die Deutsche Bibliothek verzeichnet diese Publikation in der Deutschen Nationalbibliografie; detaillierte bibliografische Daten sind im Internet über http://dnb.d-nb.de/ abrufbar.

1. Auflage 2013
Copyright © 2013 GRIN Verlag GmbH
http://www.grin.com
Druck und Bindung: Books on Demand GmbH, Norderstedt Germany
ISBN 978-3-656-39235-4

The Distributional Effect of Social Welfare Spending in an Economy: Evidence from Thailand.

Joseph Ato Forson

PhD Student
Graduate School of Public Administration, National Institute of Development Administration
(NIDA) 118 Moo3, Seree thai Road, Klong Chan, Bangkapi, Bangkok 10240 Thailand

Abstract

This paper attempts to test the validity of public welfare spending theories (compensation theory, system theory, median voter theory, group theory, Incrementalism and some variants of public choice theory) in the context of Thailand. The study make use of GDP, previous welfare spending, increases in population, tax revenue, openness to trade, democratic government, labour union, trade association, urbanisation and welfare spending as a share of GDP over the period 1982 - 2007. We found strong and positive link between globalisation, GDP, tax revenue, labour union and previous welfare spending with Thailand welfare spending. These increases will invariably call for increased access to education, health care systems and other related welfare spending which means, the revenue base has to be increased through tax. We therefore recommend Thai Government to undertake reform in the tax system to broaden the tax net. Also, land and property tax systems ought to be reformed as well to extend coverage. We also recommend the stimulation of domestic demand in Thailand to reduce the over reliance on the international market which exposes countries to high end risks and uncertainties. The falling population growth in Thailand could also spell a doom to Thai's labour supply. Thailand currently relies on immigrant workers from neigbouring countries like Myanmar, Laos, Vietnam and Burma. As the economic conditions in these countries improve, these immigrant workers might return. This will create a shortage in the supply needs to cater for the ever increasing demand propelled by the continuous industralisation of the Thai economy. Policy decision makers should factor this in their subsequent decision to mitigate this effect in the near future.

Key words: Welfare Spending; Thailand; Public Welfare spending theories.

1. Introduction

Government's role over the past decades has been to create an enabling environment with equal opportunities to all to ensure equity in all facet of life. Opponents of government direct involvement with market have always had the belief in the self-correcting mechanism of the market towards equilibrium position. However, such believe in sole mechanism of the forces of demand and supply in the market has not worked to perfection, hence the inevitable involvement of government in correcting the market inefficiency. Welfare spending on education, health, unemployment and other social transfers are some of the means government uses in forestalling confidence in the economy and to bridge the gap between the rich and the poor. Literature abound on

governments interventions through welfare spending. For instance, there are studies on the effect of social transfers/spending on growth (see Landau (1985), Korpi (1985), McCallum and Blais (1987), Persson and Tabellini (1994) Agel et al (1999) and most recently Peter Lindert (2004)[1]. These studies have indicated conflicting results of positive and negative findings on these effects, hence making it difficult to conclude on the specific gains of welfare spending especially when making a generalized conclusion. There have also been instances of some countries where social spending have discouraged productivity and aided in inducing people to be addictive especially in Sweden and Finland in the 1990s.

Thai government has made a strong commitment in bringing majority of the population from the clout of hard core poverty by expanding its social spending in increasing access to education, health care, and other welfare services. Government policy to roll out programs such as the extension of coverage of universal basic education, student loan schemes and social security benefits are among the leading government interventions in fighting inequality and poverty in Thailand. However, such a move has sparked a number of questions as to who the actual beneficiaries of government interventions are. Will government social welfare spending benefit the poor or the rich? If yes, how? Will such move stimulate or decrease economic growth? On the fiscal side, won't such move cause an increase in public debt? What other counter measures will Thai government put in place to prevent people from developing addictive inclination to these welfare programs? These and others will be the bedrock to this research program.

2. Research Questions

In a nutshell, this research will seek to find answers to the following questions;
- What are the factors affecting the growth of government welfare spending in Thailand?
- Who are the actual beneficiaries of Thai Government social Welfare spending?
- What are some of the counter measures put in place to discourage Thai people from developing social addictiveness to government social welfare spending?

2.1 Research Objectives

This research seeks to achieve two main objectives;
I.   To study the factors affecting the growth of government spending in Thailand from the period 1982 to 2007.
II. To test the validity of welfare spending theories in Thailand
III. To make recommendations based on the results of the empirical findings to the Thai Government.

3. Literature Review

Literature on social welfare spending in most research has been built from two different conceptions; the demand side theory and the supply side theory. The demand side-theory is based on traditional democratic theory that is based on the assumption that government tends to act as an agent that carries out the will or demand of the

---

[1] Cited from Peter Lindert's (2004) paper " Welfare spending hardly affect growth"

people. Government, by this is considered to be neutral and altruistic agent that responds to the needs of the society. Government spending is skewed to these demands. The supply side-theory is the opposite of the demand side-theory. Under the supply side-theory, government tends to satisfy their own whims and caprices and that spending is based on these self-centered interests of government and not the masses per se. Factors under the supply side-theory includes the ability to raise taxes, the strength of the bureaucracy, elections and parliamentary politics.

Several theories can be classified under the demand side. Most notable ones include *Wagner's law* developed by Adolph Wagner (1985), a German sociologist more than one hundred years ago. Wagner believes that there are several reasons why public expenditure including social spending tends to increase over time. Wagner argued that, *industrialization*, *urbanization* and increased *population density* would give a need for more provision of public facilities like roads, housing, hospitals and other infrastructures. In addition, economic growth and income would facilitate certain income-elastic demands such as demand for education and the redistribution of income. To test the validity of this claim by Wagner's law, three variables have been selected and applied in the estimation model.

Another theory used to explain social spending aside Wagner's law is the *public choice theory* with variants such as the Median voter theory and the demand for income distribution developed by Anthony Downs (1957), A.H. Meltzer (1981) and S.F. Richard (1983). The theory believes that in order for government to win election, must try to respond to the demands of the voter. Government spending increases when the franchise is increased to include more voters below the median income (the decisive voter) when the growth of incomes provides revenues for increased redistribution and when the income distribution becomes more uneven. Researchers often use the rate of voter turnout as the measure of median voter participation. However, in this research, due to the unavailability of such data, we made use of a proxy using *the ratio of the GDP of the nonagricultural sector* to measure economic inequality with the expectation that majority of the poor in Thailand live in the agricultural sector and are active voters.

Interest group theory has also been used to explain the social welfare spending of government. The activities of interest groups such as trade and labour associations through campaign contribution and lobbying can exert influence on legislations concerning taxes, tariffs, price ceilings and regulations. Robert D. McCormick and Robert E. Tollison (1981) in the US for instance found that the state of economic regulation varied directly with the number of trade associations registered in the state. Evidence from the European context have been provided by Tom W. Rice suggesting that interest groups are able to induce governments to introduce social programs to offset the hardship which invariably explains the growth of government expenditure between 1950 to 1980. This study will test the validity of this assertion by making use of data on the *percentage increase in the number of labour unions* in Thailand as a measure of interest groups.

Proponents of the *compensation theory* contend that globalisation has an influence on public spending. Studies by Dani Rodrick (1998), and Robert Kaufman (2001), and Alex Segura Ubiergo, and Geoffrey Garrett (2001) have all shown that globalisation have increased government interventions in the economy which have invariable increased government spending on social programs. *Globalisation* has been defined as the integration of markets (i.e. domestic and international). Countries with

high exposure to international trade will experience social dislocation. The fluctuation in export and import creates economic instability, unequal income distribution and unemployment problems. The situation will prompt government to increase spending on those affected and are disadvantaged. The need to retrain affected labour to reposition them in the competitive market will facilitate spending on education and labour training programs. In this study, trade openness (measured as *exports and imports as a percentage of GDP*) has been used to test the validity of this assertion.

When the argument is expounded from the supply side also brings to the fore a number of theories. James M. Buchanan (1975), Louise Marshall (1986), and Wallace E. Oates (1988) proposed the so-called *fiscal illusion theory* (which is a variant of public choice theory). The fiscal illusion theory believes that government has preferences for expanding its public spending. These preferences for larger budgets (social budgets) are said to be due to the need to satisfy the increasing demand of the voters. To be able to meet these preferences, government must increase taxes. However, this act may cause dissatisfaction among voters. To reduce this dissatisfaction, government tries to collect taxes that are less visible (indirect) to the tax payer as they may have less information to estimate the burden of such taxes. Succinctly, the fiscal illusion theory argues if tax burden can be disguised in this way, the government can increase public expenditure without causing dissatisfaction among voters. To prove this theory, *tax revenue as a percentage of GDP* will be used to test the validity of this theory.

Charles E. Lindblom's (1959) *Incrementalism theory* views public spending as a continuation of past spending with only incremental modifications. The theory believes that due to constraints such as time, resources and information, policy makers are unable to investigate all available alternatives in existing policy due to countless uncertainties/risks involved. Rather, preference is given to decision made on an incremental basis, where the present will slightly change from the past year(s) as the previous year is used as the base year. Incrementalism provides a good explanation for government spending. The previous year spending is a good predictor of next year's spending. To prove this theory, *one year lagged welfare expenditure as a percentage of total expenditure* is used in this research.

Political business cycle theory holds that business cycle can be artificially created by government in an electioneering year as a result of the competition for votes. Evidence to buttress this theory has been provided by Martin Paldam (1997) and Alberto Alesina and N. Roubini (1992). That is during election year, government tends to increase spending which stimulates the economy to drive demand high which induces high economic growth and reduce unemployment to satisfy the electorate/voters to gain advantage. This action tends to cause a business cycle. To test if this theory holds, the year of election (dummy variable, 1 in the year before and the year of the election, 0 in the other years) in a *democratic government* is used as the predictor of the growth of education, health and welfare spending.

4. Conceptual Framework

Based on the above literature review, and the arguments of the various theories propounded in support of government welfare spending, these variables have been identified to be key and critical in our bid to draw a conceptual framework. The essence of this section is to make visible the specific variables used and how they assume in terms of their relationship among competing variables. In line with this point, the framework below has been developed. The independent variables are presented on the left and the dependant variable on the right.

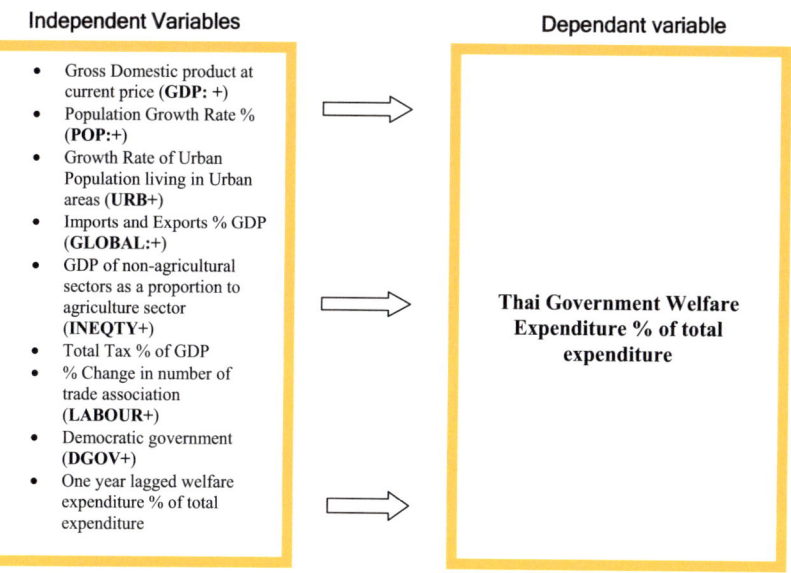

Independent Variables

- Gross Domestic product at current price (**GDP: +**)
- Population Growth Rate % (**POP:+**)
- Growth Rate of Urban Population living in Urban areas (**URB+**)
- Imports and Exports % GDP (**GLOBAL:+**)
- GDP of non-agricultural sectors as a proportion to agriculture sector (**INEQTY+**)
- Total Tax % of GDP
- % Change in number of trade association (**LABOUR+**)
- Democratic government (**DGOV+**)
- One year lagged welfare expenditure % of total expenditure

Dependant variable

Thai Government Welfare Expenditure % of total expenditure

Source: Forson (2013)

4.1 Hypothesis Testing

As evidence from the above conceptual framework, there is a relationship between the independent and dependant variable. The various theories have one way or the other postulated these relationships. We, on the basis of this have the following as the hypotheses awaiting their testability.

H_0: Urbanisation, Population growth and GDP have a positive link with government welfare spending

H_1: The ratio of the GDP of the nonagricultural to the agriculture (Inequality) is expected to have a positive relationship with government Welfare spending

H₂: the percentage increases in the number of labour unions in Thailand have a positive relationship with education, public and welfare spending

H₃: Globalisation is expected to have a positive relationship with education, public health and welfare spending

H₄: tax revenue as % of GDP is expected to have positive relationship with government welfare spending

H₅: one year lagged welfare spending is expected to have a positive relationship with current social welfare spending

H₆: A positive relationship is expected between the year of election and social welfare spending

5. Research Methodology

5.1 Data Collection

Data for this research have been provided from secondary unofficial source for the sake of simulation. However, alternatively, data for these variables can equally be gathered from primary source through a survey or a secondary source through government approved data bureau in Thailand. Since our interest is to know what factors are responsible for government social spending over a period of time (1982-2007), it will be better to collect such data from government sources.

5.2 Model Specification and Data Analysis

We began our data analysis by checking for multicollinearity. A correlation matrix among the variable was one of the straightforward ways of dealing with this problem. We found high correlation among certain variables. In statistical literature, correlation among variables should not exceed 0.8. The higher they are, there is the tendency that the variables are measuring the same thing so one has to be dropped/deleted. Another solution is to separate the highly correlated variables from a given model and then have them run separately in a different equation.

Based on the conceptual framework developed and the hypothesis formulated, the regression model equation will assume this form;

Model 1:

$GWEL = a + b_1GDP + b_2POP + b_3URB + b_4GLOBAL + b_5INEQTY + b_6REV + b_7TRADE + b_8LABOUR + b_9DGOV + b_{10}GWEL_{t-1} + e$

Where, *e* is the *error term* of the model equation. All other variables have already been defined in the conceptual frame in section 4 above.

We, by this model equation test for multicollinearity and try to resolve the problem that may arise. Table 1 below is the correlation matrix.

Table 1: CORRELATION MATRIX OF ALL VARIABLES

	GLOBAL	INEQTY	REV	DGOV	GDP	POP	URB	TRADE	LOBOUR	GWEL-1	GWEL
GLOBAL	1.00										
INEQTY	0.71	1.00									
REV	0.87	0.94	1.00								
DGOV	0.57	0.72	0.64	1.00							
GDP	0.97	0.77	0.90	0.54	1.00						
POP	-0.74	-0.72	-0.78	-0.49	-0.75	1.00					
URB	0.61	0.16	0.38	0.08	0.58	-0.06	1.00				
TRADE	-0.38	-0.20	-0.26	-0.22	-0.39	0.23	-0.36	1.00			
LOBOR	0.96	0.82	0.94	0.62	0.95	-0.78	0.48	-0.37	1.00		
GWEL-1	0.95	0.76	0.87	0.55	0.94	-0.73	0.55	-0.49	0.94	1.00	
GWEL	0.95	0.83	0.94	0.60	0.94	-0.76	0.47	-0.39	0.99	0.95	1.00

Note: Table 1 is the correlation matrix of all our variables (both dependant and independent). In order to check serial correlation to resolve the problem of multicollinearity, we have correlated all variables in a matrix. The results indicate some variables are highly correlated[2].

To resolve this problem, we have decided to separate some of the variables to give different model equations for easy regression as shown below;

Model 2:
GWEL= a + b_1GDP +b_2POP +b_3URB + b_4 REV + e

Model 3:
GWEL= a + b_1GLOBAL +b_2DGOV + e

Model 4:
GWEL= a + b_1INEQTY +b_2 DGOV + e

Model 5:
GWEL= a + b_1TRADE +b_2LABOUR + e

Model 6:
GWEL= a + b_1GWEL$_{t-1}$ + e

---

[2] In statistical literature, correlation among variables should not be more than 0.8. The higher they are, the more they measure the same thing. It is recommended we either delete those items, or have them separated in different equations

6. Empirical Results

The empirical findings from the multiple regressions can be summarized for the dependant variable as follows;

Table 2: Results of Multiple regression of Model 2- 4 (**Dependant variable: Welfare Spending**)

Variables	Model 2			Model 3			Model 4		
	Coefficients (β)	T	P	Coefficients (β)	T	P	Coefficients (β)	T	P
Constant	-1.733	.787	.440	4.732**	18.001	0	3.409**	4.317	0
GDP	0.548**	2.86	0.009						
REV	0.487**	3.60	0.002						
POP	0.034	0.284	0.779						
URB	-0.025	-0.253	0.803						
GLOBAL				0.892**	11.444	0			
DGOV				0.098	1.255	0.222	0	0	1
INEQTY							0.832**	4.958	0
TRADE									
LABOUR									
GWEL (t-1)									
N	26			26			26		
R^2	0.94			0.905			0.692		
adjusted R^2	0.93			0.897			0.666		
F	80.58			109.429			25.872		
p	0.000			0.000			0.000		

Note: *standardized coefficient (β)*
*Statistically significant at 0.05 level.
**Statistically Significant at 0.01 level.

In Model 2, the regression is done to prove the validity of Wagner law and system theory that argues that government spending on social welfare is based on reasons such as the need to satisfy increasing population, urbanisation, tax revenue and GDP growth. In model 2, two of the variables selected are seen to be positive and statistically significant. GDP and Tax revenue recorded positive effects on Thai government welfare spending. This implies, as the economy of Thailand expands or grows, its spillover effect is positively felt on individual incomes which rises to reflect the market expansion, government tax revenue will accordingly increase as the taxation system in Thailand is progressive. For instance, given a constant, the contribution of GDP growth to welfare spending will be 0.548 percent whiles that of tax revenue will be 0.487 percent all things being equal. However, on the other two variables (URB and POP) were insignificant. Population increase had a positive coefficient implying a positive association with welfare spending but insignificant. Urbanization's contribution to welfare spending is also weak as shown. That is, as population increases, the need to provide education, health care systems become important in Thailand. However, the case in Thailand might be different as population was insignificant and the population trend is rather falling (*see figure 1 below*). Possible reason could be, population growth in Thailand could either be falling, steady or constant thereby not warranty increases in government's welfare spending. Additionally, population growth is seen to have a direct link with urbanisation which was all insignificant. Government policy in Thailand in general is pro-poor so less

attention is given to the rich who are in the urbanized centers. This could be a possible reason why welfare spending on urbanisation is low and insignificant. Perhaps, Thai people are increasingly becoming conscious of birth controls measures, as evident in urbanized and big cities. This mirrors how modernized and infiltrated the Thai system has been subjected to by the globalisation waves from western countries where birth rates have continuously remained stagnant and even falling. The latter finding in Thailand doesn't support Wagner's law for these two variables. In general, the model explains 92.7 percent of the cross variable variations. This is high by all standards.

Figure 1: Trend of Population and Urbanisation in Thailand (1982-2007)

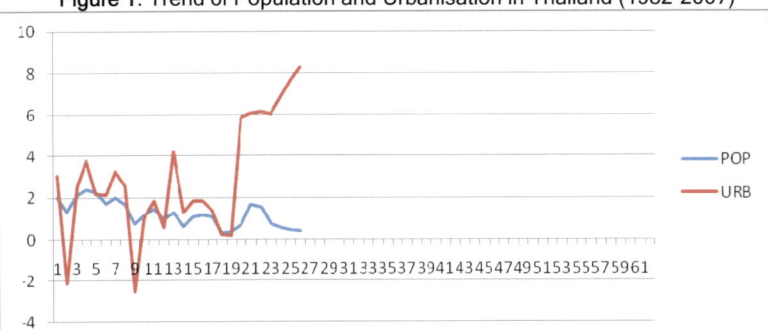

Source: Author's construct, 2013.
Note: Graphical presentation of data on population and urbanisation trend in Thailand over the period 1982-2007. The trend for population indicates a fall but urbanisation is rising steadily in Thailand.

Model 3 regresses welfare spending on democratic government and globalization. This is to test the validity of compensation theory. From table 3, globalisation proxied by trade openness in Thailand is seen to be statistically significant with positive coefficient. It contributes 0.892 percent to welfare spending in Thailand. The constant in the model is highly significant at 0.005 as well. This implies, given a 4.73 percent rise in total government welfare spending as a percentage of GDP, spending to cater for highly hit sector of the Thai economy as a result of globalisation fluctuation will account for 0.892 percent of the total allocation. This is in support of compensation theory which states that countries opened to domestic and international trades are highly exposed to the risks and uncertainties that may erupt as a result of global fluctuations. Governments tend to increase social welfare spending in such times to cater for the disadvantaged. Spending on education through retraining of affected labour to make them competitive for an alternative job market becomes inevitable. Model 3 explains 89.7 of the cross variable variations, which is quite credible and acceptable.

Model 4 regresses welfare spending on inequality and democratic government. The result shows a statistically significant relation between inequality and welfare spending. This can be interpreted to mean, welfare spending on inequality in Thailand is high. It accounts for 0.832 percent of welfare spending given a constant of 3.41 percent

of government's total spending on welfare as a share of GDP. This finding supports the argument of median voter theory that says government tends to be responsive to the demands of the poor who are the marginalized in the society who constitute majority of the franchised voters. On the other hand, democratic government was insignificant as the focus has always been on the inequality group. Whether the government system is democratic or military/autocratic, the underlying factor is to hold on to power and that comes about by meeting the demands of this inequality/marginalized group in the society. Model 4 explanatory power is relatively low (about 67 percent), implying the model doesn't have all the explanation to this model. Other variables that are not represented in this model might possibly explain this cross variable variation. There is the need to explore what these variables are in order to improve the explanatory power of this model.

Table 3: Results of Multiple regression of Model 5- 6 (**Dependant variable: Welfare Spending**)

Variables	Model 5			Model 6		
	Coefficients (β)	T	P	Coefficients (β)	T	P
Constant	-3.948**	-9.968	0	0.427	0.825	0.417
GDP						
REV						
POP						
URB						
GLOBAL						
DGOV						
INEQTY						
TRADE	-0.034	-1.162	0.257			
LABOUR	0.979**	33.83	0			
GWEL (t-1)				0.954**	15.571	0
N	26			26		
R^2	0.983			0.91		
adjusted R^2	0.982			0.906		
F	678.588			242.455		
p	0.000			0.000		

Note: Standardized coefficient (β)
*Statistically significant at 0.05 level.
**Statistically Significant at 0.01 level.

In model 5, welfare spending is regressed on trade and labour. Labour union has a statistically positive relationship with welfare spending with a coefficient of 0.979 percent. This finding supports interest group theory. This underscores the strength of labour union/association in Thailand (*see figure 2*). These associations can influence legislature through campaign contribution and lobbying for increased welfare spending. On the contrary, trade associations in Thailand have a weaker link on welfare spending. This also underscores weak influence of trade unions and their existence in Thailand. Trade associations are not vibrant in Thailand as shown in figure 2 below. On the whole, the explanatory power or fitness of this model is extremely high (about 98 percent).

Figure 2: Trend of Trade Union and Labour association in Thailand (1982-2007)

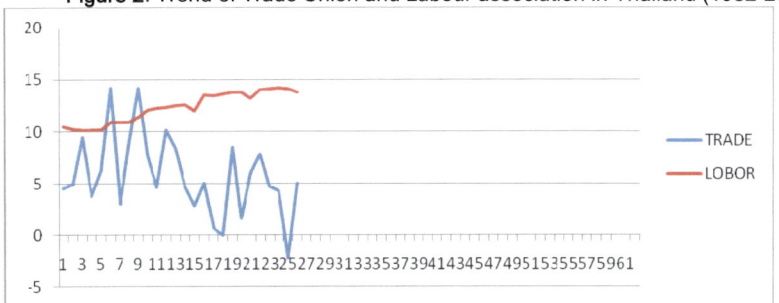

Source: Author's construct,2013.

In model 6, welfare spending is regressed on a constant and welfare spending of the previous year. The lagged welfare spending is seen to be highly significant with a positive coefficient of 0.954 percent. This finding also supports the theories of Incrementalism and budget maximizing bureaucrat that contends that public welfare spending should be a continuation of past spending with only incremental modifications due to time and resource constraint of investigating all of their alternatives in existing policy. Additionally, bureaucrats may demand such increment in budget for their personal needs and interest and not that of the citizens, interest groups or legislators. This big budget can be used for high salary, leisure and high public reputation and power. The fitness of this model is high as it accounts for about 90 percent of the explanation in this model.

7. Policy Recommendation

On the basis of the above empirical results, the following policy recommendations have been put forward on both the demand and supply sides;

Globalisation has a strong significant influence on social spending in Thailand due to greater exposure to international market which has tended to increased spending on education, health and welfare spending. Similarly, there is a positive demand effect by Inequality, labour unions, revenue on taxes and GDP growth for the same welfare spending on education, health care etc. These increases in the demand for social spending imply a need for growing revenues in Thailand.

We recommend a reform in the tax system in Thailand by broadening the income tax base and reforms in land and property tax. This will increase the revenue of Thai government to meet these increasing demands on education, health and welfare spending.

We also recommend Thai government to put up measures that will stimulate domestic demand to gradually reduce the effects of global fluctuations. Additionally, Thai government welfare spending should address the needs of the majority of the rural poor whose mainstay are agriculture and its allied occupation. The falling population growth in Thailand could also spell a doom to Thai's labour supply. Thailand currently relies on immigrant workers from neigbouring countries like Myanmar, Laos, Vietnam and Burma. As the economic conditions in these countries improve, these immigrant

workers might return. This will create a shortage in the supply needs to cater for the ever increasing demand propelled by the continuous industralisation of the Thai economy. Policy decision makers should factor in this in subsequent decision to mitigate this effect in the near future.

Last but not least, we also recommend a pragmatic approach to the notion of development as opposed to the positivists approach using GDP as the measure of well-being which has not been felt by the masses. From the data, inequality in Thailand keeps widening irrespective of the consistent expansion of the economy (GDP). The poor have become poorer whiles the rich are becoming richer. The development focus should tune in to the one that will put the development of the masses at the forefront. The big numbers must be reflected in the betterment of the rural poor by enhancing their opportunities in living a sustained life.

Acknowledgement
I am very grateful to Prof. Pornlapat Buracom, the lecturer for Fiscal and Monetary Policy Analysis and Management (DA 841), at the National Institute of Development Administration (NIDA). This research program would not have been possible without the well taught lectures and materials provided by Prof. Pornlapat Buracom, who doubles as the Director of International program at GSPA. The same appreciation goes to Prof. Suchitra, a co-lecturer of Quantitative Analysis for the expert work done in exposing students to the intricacies of doing a good quantitative research with SPSS. This research program would not have also been possible without the contribution of my colleagues in class. To the Teaching Assistant, Mr. Rodwell from Malawi, I say big thank you for the information and additional insight shed on the course. I also wish to acknowledge the endless efforts of the PhD administrative staffs of GSPA for their excellent administrative contributions to making this course a success.

REFERENCE

Aaron Wildavsky (1964), "*the politics of budgetary process*" Boston, little brown.

Adolph Wagner (1985), "*Finanzwissenschaft*," in Classics in the theory of public finance, ed. Richard Musgraveand Allan Peacoook, 23-46, Macmillan.

Alberto Alesina and N. Roubini, (1992) "political *business cycles in OECD Economies*", review of economic studies 59, no.2: 669

Charles E. Lindblom (1959), "*the science of Muddling through*", public administration review 19, no.1, 26-34.

Dani Rodrik (1998)," *why do more open economies have bigger government?*" journal of political economy 106, no.2: 997.

James M. Buchanan (1975), *the limits of liberty*, university of Chicago press

Louise Marshall (1991), "*new evidence of fiscal illusion: the 1986 tax*", American economic review 81 No.2, 1339.

Martin Paldam (1997), "*the political business cycle*", in perspective in public choice, ed. Cambridge university press

Pornlapat Buracom (2011), "*the determinants and distributional effects of public education, health and welfare spending in Thailand*", Asian Affairs: an American review vol.38, no.3, 113

Thomas E. Borccherding (1977), "*budgets and bureaucrats: the sources of government growth*". Duke university press

Wallace E. Oates, (1988) "*on the nature and measurement of fiscal illusion: a survey*" in taxation and fiscal federalism, ed. Geoffrey Brennan 81, Australian national university press.

APPENDIX:
DATA ON SOCIAL WELFARE SPENDING IN THAILAND (1982-2007)

Year	GLOBAL	INEQTY	REV	DGOV	GDP	POP	URB	TRADE	LOBOR	GWEL$_{t-1}$	GWEL
1982	43.46	4.26	13.9	0	0.82	2.03	3.04	4.54	10.4	7.1	6.4
1983	42.09	4.62	13.6	0	0.91	1.36	-2.2	4.97	10.2	6.4	6.3
1984	43.19	4.49	13.6	0	0.97	2.16	2.5	9.47	10.1	6.3	6.3
1985	43.82	5.01	13.8	0	1.01	2.4	3.77	3.78	10.1	6.3	6.4
1986	43.34	4.76	13.8	0	1.09	2.27	2.19	6.25	10.1	6.4	6.4
1987	50.6	5.02	13.9	0	1.23	1.71	2.14	14.21	10.9	6.4	6.5
1988	60.83	5.15	13.9	1	1.46	2.02	3.27	3	10.9	6.5	6.5
1989	66.39	6.01	14	1	1.69	1.69	2.55	8.75	10.9	6.5	6.6
1990	70.34	7.7	15.5	1	2.91	0.74	-2.5	14.18	11.4	6.6	7.2
1991	71.7	8.23	16	0	2.5	1.17	1.01	7.72	12.1	7.2	8
1992	72.52	9.01	16.1	1	2.83	1.45	1.85	4.67	12.2	8	8.1
1993	80.2	9.51	16.5	1	3.17	0.95	0.57	10.12	12.3	8.1	8.5
1994	82.6	9.56	16.7	1	3.63	1.3	4.21	8.38	12.5	8.5	8.7
1995	90.4	9.64	16.9	1	4.18	0.62	1.28	4.74	12.6	8.7	8.9
1996	84.8	9.75	16	1	4.61	1.1	1.82	2.86	12	8.9	8
1997	94.6	9.75	16.9	1	4.73	1.16	1.83	5.09	13.5	8	9.6
1998	101.9	8.7	16	1	4.62	1.07	1.35	0.66	13.4	9.6	9.6
1999	104	8.9	16.3	1	4.63	0.32	0.21	0	13.6	9.6	9.7
2000	124.9	8.71	16.6	1	4.92	0.35	0.17	8.53	13.8	9.7	9.8
2001	125.3	8.61	16.6	1	5.13	0.7	5.85	1.61	13.8	9.8	9.8
2002	121.7	9	16.4	1	5.44	1.67	6.08	5.95	13.2	9.8	9.6
2003	124.6	8.61	17	1	5.93	1.56	6.15	7.86	14	9.6	10
2004	136.5	8.7	17.1	1	5.79	0.76	6.04	4.69	14.1	10	10.1
2005	148.3	8.74	17.2	1	6.32	0.59	6.8	4.31	14.2	10.1	10.2
2006	143.9	8.38	17.1	1	6.96	0.45	7.66	-2.23	14.1	10.2	10.1
2007	138.5	8.29	16.8	0	7.6	0.41	8.28	5.04	13.8	10.1	9.8